CARPENTRY
ESSENTIALS

D1279824

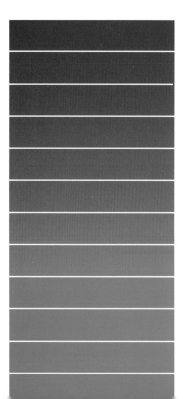

COWLES
Creative Publishing

A Division of Cowles Enthusiast Media, Inc.

Credits

Copyright © 1996
Cowles Creative Publishing, Inc.
Formerly Cy DeCosse Incorporated
5900 Green Oak Drive
Minnetonka, Minnesota 55343
1-800-328-3895
All rights reserved
Printed in U.S.A.

COWLES
Creative Publishing
A Division of Cowles Enthusiast Media, Inc.

President/COO: Nino Tarantino
Executive V.P./Editor-in-Chief: William B. Jones

Created by: The Editors of Cowles Creative Publishing, Inc., in cooperation with Black & Decker. ●BLACK&DECKER is a trademark of the Black & Decker Corporation and is used under license.

Printed on American paper by:
 Quebecor Printing
 99 98 97 96 / 5 4 3 2 1

COWLES
Enthusiast Media

President/COO: Philip L. Penny

Books available in this series:

Wiring Essentials
Plumbing Essentials
Carpentry Essentials
Painting Essentials
Flooring Essentials
Landscape Essentials
Masonry Essentials
Door & Window Essentials
Roof System Essentials
Deck Essentials
Porch & Patio Essentials
Built-In Essentials

Contents

Framing square

C-clamp

Plumb bob/
chalk line

Nail
sets

16-oz. claw hammer

Phillips screwdriver

Standard screwdriver

Mallet

Sanding
block

2' carpenter's level

Putty
knife

Chisel

Utility
knife

STUDSENSOR II

Electronic
stud
finder

BLACK&DECKER
Professional

³⁄₈'' power
drill

Drill bits

T-bevel

Cordless
screwdriver

Combination
square

Cat's
paw

12' tape
measure

Wonderbar®

STANLEY

STANLEY
Dry Wall Saw
No.15-207 6 1/2POINTS
U.S.A.

Wallboard
saw

Crosscut
saw

Starter tool set should include a generous selection of hand tools, plus a ³⁄₈-inch power drill and a cordless screwdriver. Inspect the finish on hand tools. Quality hand tools made of high-carbon steel are machined with clean-cut metal surfaces. Tool handles should be tight and comfortably molded.

Tool Basics

A quality tool collection does not require a large initial investment. A home owner can build a tool collection by buying tools as they are needed for each carpentry project. Invest in top-grade tools made by reputable manufacturers. A quality tool always carries a full parts and labor warranty.

Read power tool specifications to compare features like horsepower, motor speed and cutting capacity. Better-quality tools also have roller or ball bearings instead of sleeve bearings, reinforced power cords, and heavy-duty trigger switches.

Intermediate tool collection includes additional power tools and special-purpose hand tools. Replace blades or resharpen cutting tools whenever they become dull.

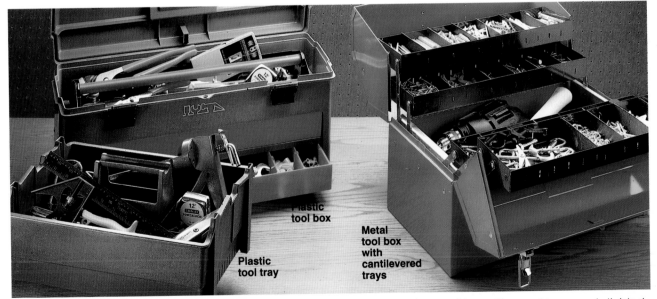

Tool boxes made of plastic or metal are lightweight and durable. Tool boxes with cantilevered trays and divided compartments keep tools and materials organized.

Measuring & Layout Tools

An important first step in every carpentry project is measuring distances and angles accurately. Buy a steel tape measure with a ¾-inch-wide blade for general home use.

A combination square is a compact tool used to measure and mark 45° and 90° angles. Use a framing square to lay out 90° angles. Choose a T-bevel with a locking handle to measure and transfer any angle.

To check surfaces for plumb and level, buy a quality 2-foot carpenter's level made of metal or wood. Select a level with screw-in bubble vials that can be replaced if they are damaged. Also buy a string chalk line to lay out long, straight lines.

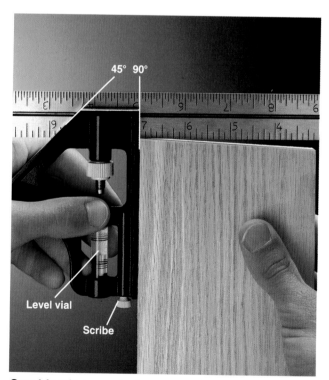

Steel tape measure with ¾-inch-wide blade is good for general-purpose home use. Choose a tape with blade marked every 16" for easy layout of stud or joist locations.

Combination square is many tools in one. The adjustable handle has two straight surfaces for marking 90° and 45° angles. The square also has a built-in level. Some squares include a pointed metal scribe to mark work for cutting.

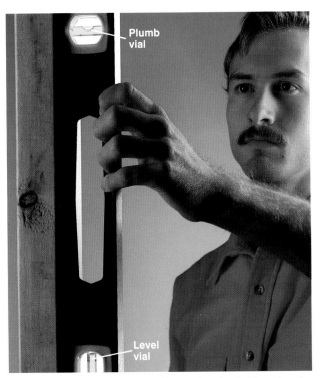

Plumb
vial

Level
vial

Two-foot carpenter's level has plumb vial for checking vertical surfaces and a level vial for checking horizontal surfaces. Level shows correct position when bubble is exactly between the line markings.

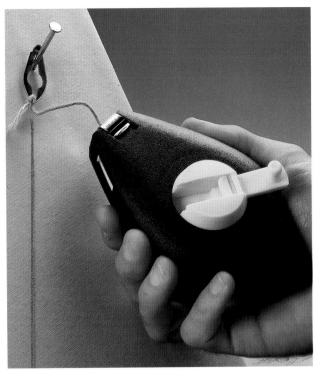

Chalk line marks long lines needed for large layout jobs. Hold string taut at both ends, and snap firmly to mark surface. Chalk line can also be used as a plumb bob for laying out stud walls.

How to Duplicate Angles with a T-bevel

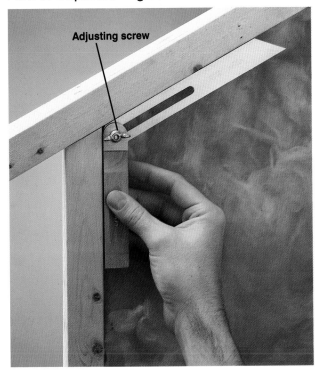

Adjusting screw

1 Loosen the T-bevel adjusting screw and adjust the arms to match the angle to be copied. Tighten the adjusting screw.

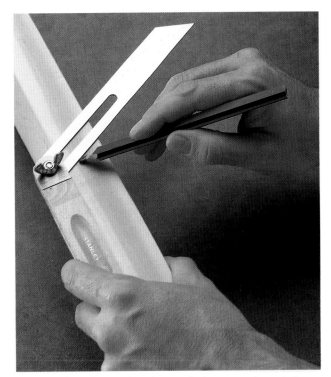

2 Move the T-bevel to the workpiece, and mark the profile of the angle. Cut the workpiece to match the angle.

Handsaws

Handsaws can be more practical than portable power saws for small jobs and occasional use.

The crosscut saw is a standard cutting tool designed to cut across the wood grain. A crosscut saw may also be used for occasional "rip" cuts parallel to the wood grain. A crosscut saw with 10 teeth per inch is a good choice for general-purpose cutting.

A backsaw and miter box makes straight cuts. The reinforced spine keeps the backsaw blade from flexing. The miter box locks at any angle for cutting precise miters and bevels.

A coping saw makes curved cuts on materials like wood molding. The coping saw has a very narrow, flexible blade held taut by a C-shaped spring frame. To adjust blade position for scroll cuts, rotate the spigots holding the blade.

Hacksaws are designed to cut metal. Like a coping saw, a hacksaw has a fine, flexible blade that can be replaced when it becomes dull.

Hacksaw

Coping saw

Crosscut saw

Backsaw

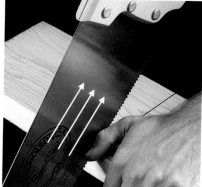

Begin handsaw cuts with upward strokes to establish the cut line, then make long, smooth strokes with blade at 45° angle to workpiece. Guide the saw at the beginning of a cut by supporting the edge with the side of your thumb.

Crosscut saw is a standard carpenter's tool. At end of cut, saw slowly and support waste material with a free hand to prevent the wood from splintering.

Backsaw with miter box cuts precise angles. Clamp or hold workpiece in miter box. Make certain that miter box is securely fastened to work surface.

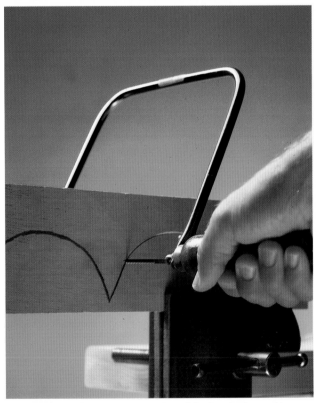

Coping saw has a thin, flexible blade designed to cut curves. It is a necessary tool for cutting and fitting wood moldings.

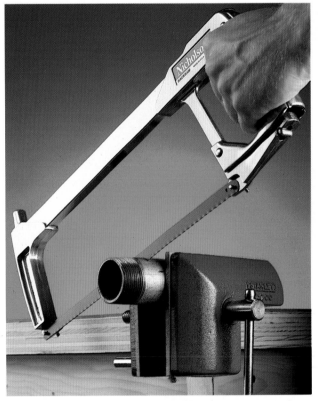

Hacksaw has a flexible, fine-tooth blade designed to cut metal. Blade must be stretched tightly in frame.

Circular Saw

The power circular saw is ideal for making fast, straight cuts in wood. Special-purpose saw blades make it possible to cut metal, plaster or even concrete with a circular saw. The locking baseplate pivots to adjust blade depth, and rotates for bevel cuts.

Choose a saw with blade size of at least 7¼ inches. A smaller saw may not cut through 2-inch lumber, especially when set at a bevel position. Select a saw with a motor rated at 2 horse-power or more.

Because a circular saw blade cuts as it rotates upward, the top face of the workpiece may splinter. To protect the finished side of the workpiece, mark measurements on back side of workpiece. Place the good side down, or facing away from the baseplate, when cutting.

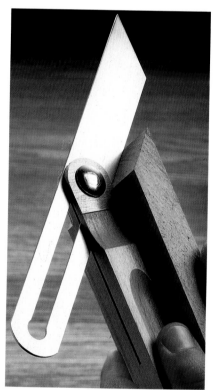

Check the cutting angle of circular saw with a T-bevel or square. Make test cuts on scrap wood. If bevel scale is inaccurate, adjust the baseplate to compensate (page opposite).

Use an edge guide for straight, long cuts. Clamp a straightedge on the workpiece. Keep baseplate tight against edge guide and move the saw smoothly.

Panel blade for smooth cuts in plywood

Hollow ground planer blade for fine woodworking

Carbide-tipped combination blade

Masonry blade

Metal-cutting blade

Precisi
Saw Blade

BLACK & D

Chro
Plated Saw

BLACK & DECKER

Piranf
Carbide-Tooth Sa

BLACK
Ab
Saw

BLACK & D
Abras
Saw Blac

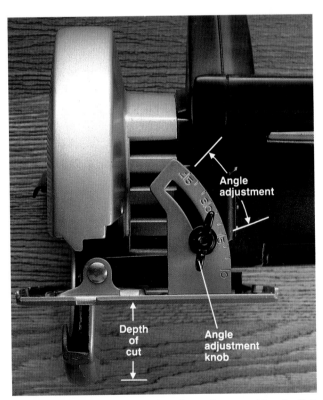

Angle adjustment

Depth of cut

Angle adjustment knob

Set blade angle by loosening the adjustment knob. Set blade depth by loosening adjustment knob at rear of saw. For safety, set the blade so that it projects through bottom of workpiece by no more than the length of one saw tooth. Tighten knobs firmly.

Circular saw blades include: carbide-tipped combination blade for general use; panel blade with small teeth which do not chip thin veneer layers in plywood; hollow-ground planer blade with tapered surface that reduces friction, used for fine woodworking; abrasive blades used to cut metal or masonry.

Jig Saw

The jig saw is the best choice for cutting curves. The cutting capacity of a jig saw depends on its power and the length of its blade stroke. Choose a saw rated to cut 2-inch-thick softwood and ¾-inch-thick hardwood stock. Some jig saws have a pivoting baseplate that can be locked to make bevel cuts.

Select a variable-speed jig saw, because different blade styles may require different cutting speeds for best results. In general, use faster blade speeds when cutting with coarse-tooth blades and slower speeds with fine-tooth blades.

A jig saw tends to vibrate because of the up-and-down blade action. A quality jig saw has a heavy-gauge steel baseplate that reduces vibration. To further minimize vibration, hold the saw tightly against the workpiece, and move the saw slowly so the blade does not bend.

Because jig saw blades cut on the upward stroke, the top side of the workpiece may splinter. If the wood has a good side to protect, cut with this surface facing downward.

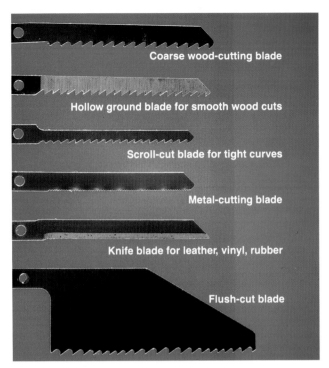

Coarse wood-cutting blade

Hollow ground blade for smooth wood cuts

Scroll-cut blade for tight curves

Metal-cutting blade

Knife blade for leather, vinyl, rubber

Flush-cut blade

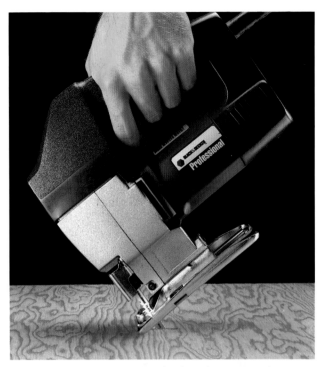

Jig saw blades come in different designs for cutting different materials. Choose a blade that is correct for the job. With fine-tooth blades that have 14 or more teeth per inch, set saw at low blade speed. Coarse blades require faster blade speeds.

Plunge cuts are made by tipping the saw so front edge of the baseplate is held firmly against workpiece. Start saw, and slowly lower it to a horizontal position, letting blade gradually cut through workpiece.

Scrolling knob

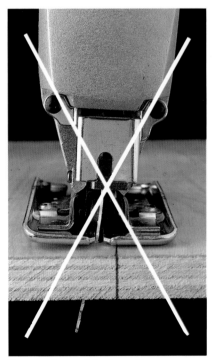

Scroll or curved cuts are made with a narrow blade. Move saw slowly to avoid bending the blade. Some jig saws have a scrolling knob that allows the blade to be turned without turning the saw.

Cut metals with a fine-tooth metal-cutting blade and select a slow blade speed. Support sheet metals with thin plywood to eliminate vibration. Use emery paper or a file to smooth burred edges left by jig saw blade.

Do not force blades. Jig saw blades are flexible and may break if forced. Move saw slowly when cutting bevels or tough materials like knots in wood.

Hammers

Hammers are made in a wide variety of sizes and shapes. Choose a hammer with a smoothly finished, high-carbon steel head and a quality handle made of hickory, fiberglass, or solid steel.

The 16-ounce curved claw hammer is the most frequently used hammer for carpentry. It is designed only for driving, setting, or pulling nails. For all other striking jobs, use a specialty hammer. A tack hammer with a magnetic head drives nails and tacks that are too small to hold. A rubber- or plastic-head mallet drives wood chisels. Select a ball peen hammer to pound hardened metal tools, like masonry chisels or pry bars, because it has a heat-treated steel head that resists chipping.

Use a nail set to drive nail heads below the work surface without damaging the wood.

Clean hammer face periodically with fine sandpaper. Wood resins and nail coatings may build up on the face, causing the hammer to slip and mar the work surface or bend the nail.

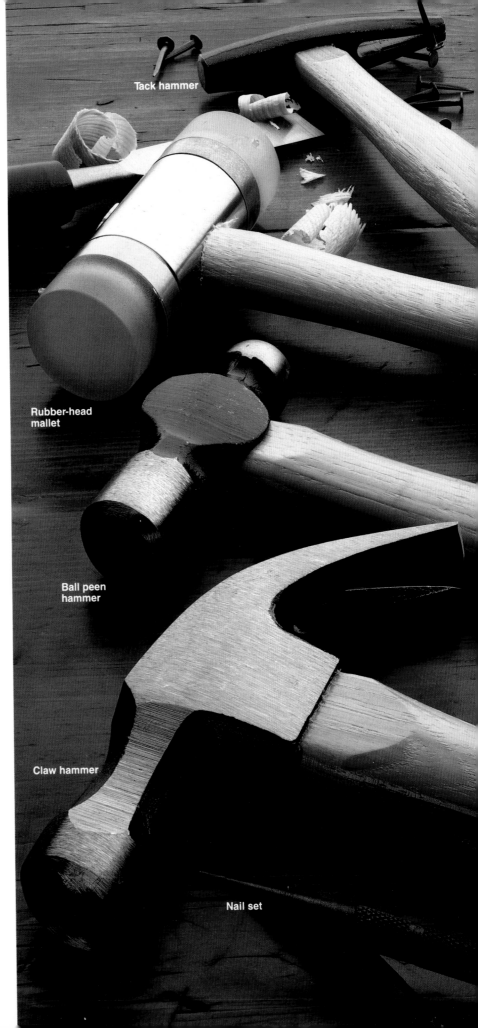

Tack hammer

Rubber-head mallet

Ball peen hammer

Claw hammer

Nail set

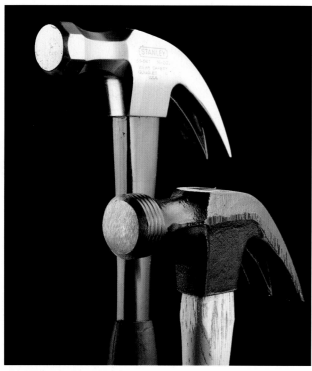

Claw hammer drives and pulls nails. Choose a quality hammer (left) with a 16-ounce head. Look for a smoothly finished, high-carbon steel head. Bargain tool (right) has rougher, painted finish with visible cast marks.

Tack hammer with magnetic head drives small nails or brads that are difficult to hold by hand.

Mallet with rubber or plastic head drives woodworking chisels. Soft mallet face will not damage fine woodworking tools.

Ball peen hammer has heat-treated steel head that resists chipping when driving hardened steel tools or pry bars.

Nail set drives heads of finish and casing nails below wood surface. Choose a nail set with tip that is slightly smaller than nail head.

Nails

The wide variety of nail styles and sizes makes it possible to choose exactly the right fastener for the job. Use either common or box nails for general framing work. Box nails are smaller in diameter, which makes them less likely to split wood. Most common and box nails have a cement or vinyl coating that improves their holding power.

Finish and casing nails have small heads and are driven just below the work surface with a nail set, for projects like nailing wood trim. Casing nails have a slightly larger head than finish nails for better holding power. Galvanized nails have a zinc coating that resists rusting, and are used for outdoor projects.

Other specialty nails are identified by their intended function, like wallboard nails, siding nails, masonry nails, or flooring nails.

Nail lengths are identified by numbers from 4 to 60 followed by the letter "d," which stands for "penny." Some specialty nails are identified by either length or gauge.

Nail Sizes

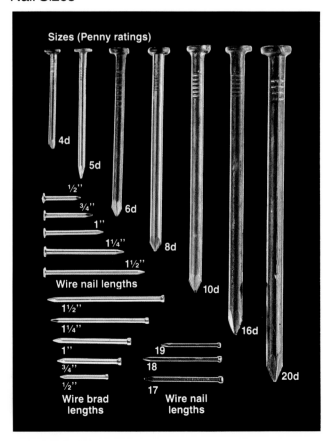

Sizes (Penny ratings)

4d
5d
6d
8d
10d
16d
20d

½"
¾"
1"
1¼"
1½"
Wire nail lengths

1½"
1¼"
1"
¾"
½"
Wire brad lengths

19
18
17
Wire nail lengths

Types of Nails

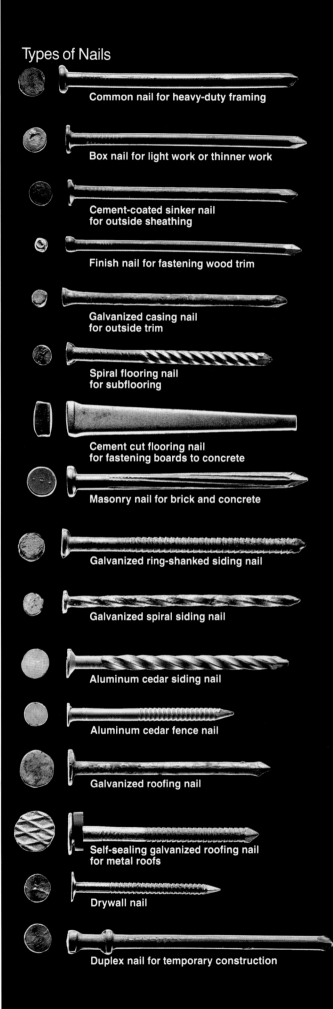

Common nail for heavy-duty framing

Box nail for light work or thinner work

Cement-coated sinker nail for outside sheathing

Finish nail for fastening wood trim

Galvanized casing nail for outside trim

Spiral flooring nail for subflooring

Cement cut flooring nail for fastening boards to concrete

Masonry nail for brick and concrete

Galvanized ring-shanked siding nail

Galvanized spiral siding nail

Aluminum cedar siding nail

Aluminum cedar fence nail

Galvanized roofing nail

Self-sealing galvanized roofing nail for metal roofs

Drywall nail

Duplex nail for temporary construction

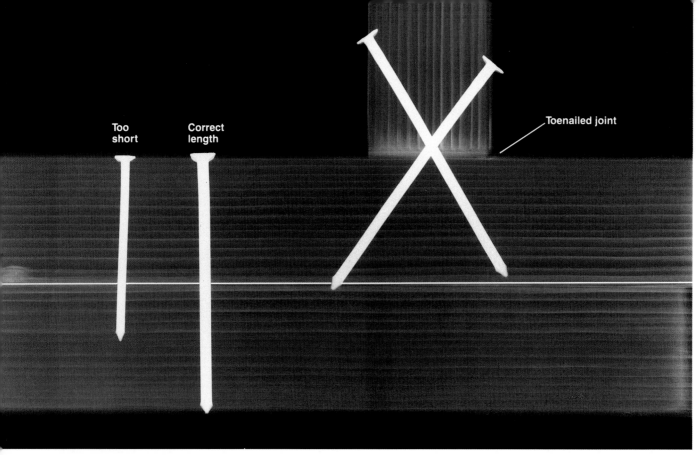

Too short | Correct length | Toenailed joint

X-ray view shows how nails penetrate wood. Longer nail that fully penetrates second 2 × 4 has greater holding power than short nail. Use toenailing (right) when nails cannot be driven from the outside surface. Drive nails at opposing 45° angles. Offset nail positions so that nails do not hit each other.

Tips for Nailing

Drive flat concrete nails into the mortar joints instead of the concrete blocks. Mortar is easier to penetrate.

Metal connectors help join wood with ease and speed, and are often used to connect studs to sole and top plates.

How to Fasten Wood to a Steel Beam

1 Coat the top of 2 × 4 with a generous application of construction adhesive. Clamp 2 × 4 to bottom of I-beam.

2 Drill holes spaced 16" on-center through 2 × 4 and base of I-beam, using ⁹⁄₆₄-inch twist bit. Use low speed when drilling metal. Drive 16d common nails through holes and clinch them on base of I-beam.

Clinch nails for extra holding power. Bend the nail over slightly, then drive it flush to the surface with a hammer.

Use finish nail in electric drill to bore a pilot hole in hardwood. Tighten drill chuck securely on nail.

Prying Tools

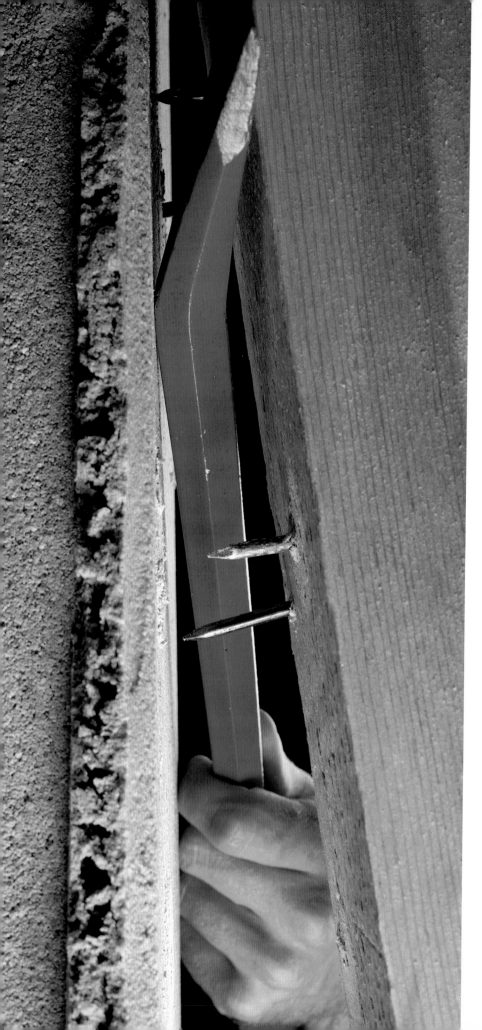

Quality pry bars are made of high-carbon steel, and are available in many sizes. Choose tools forged in a single piece. Tools made from welded parts are not as strong as those that are forged.

Most pry bars have a curved claw at one end for pulling nails and a chisel-shaped tip at the opposite end for other prying jobs. Improve leverage by placing a wood block under the head of pry tools.

Wonderbar® is a slightly flexible tool made of flattened steel. This tool is useful for a variety of prying and wrecking jobs. Both ends can be used for pulling nails.

Prying tools include wrecking bars for heavy demolition work, cat's paws for removing nails, and brad pullers. Wonderbars are made of flattened steel and come in a variety of sizes for light and heavy use.

Wrecking bar, sometimes called a crowbar, is a rigid, heavy-use tool for demolition and heavy prying jobs. Use scrap wood under the bar to protect surfaces.

Cat's paw has a sharpened claw. To extract nails, drive the claw into the wood under the nail head with a hammer.

Drills

Most drilling jobs can be done easily with a power drill. Power drills are commonly available in ¼-, ⅜- and ½-inch sizes. The number refers to the largest bit shank diameter that fits the drill chuck. A ⅜-inch drill is a good choice because it accepts a wide range of bits and accessories. A variable-speed reversing (VSR) drill will adapt to many uses, like drilling masonry, or driving and removing wallboard screws. A cordless drill offers freedom from extension cords.

When choosing a drill, look for quality features like an extra-long power cord with reinforced cord protector, and a sealed switch that prevents dirt from entering the trigger. A drill that uses top-quality materials may actually be smaller, lighter, and easier to handle than a cheaper drill.

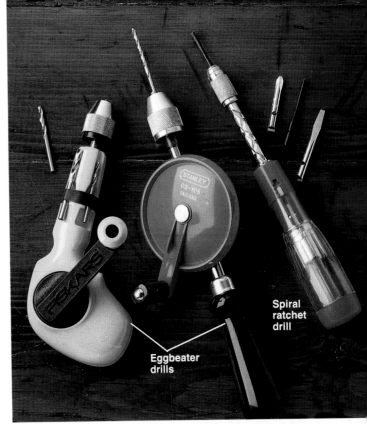

Hand drills include eggbeater and spiral ratchet styles. Hand drills are often used in fine woodworking, or for carpentry jobs where a power drill is not convenient.

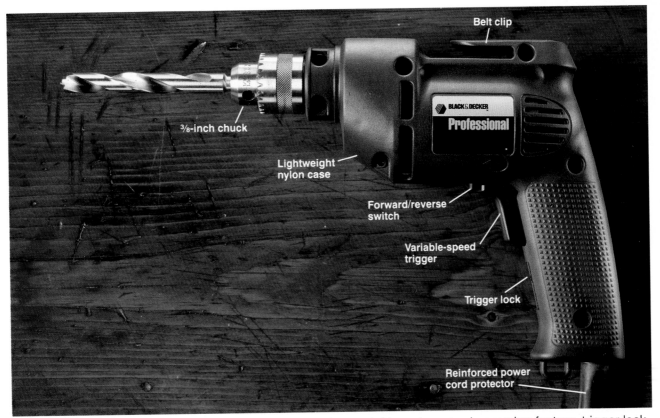

Power drill features to look for include ⅜-inch chuck size, variable motor speed, reversing feature, trigger lock to set a constant speed, a heavy power cord with reinforced protector, a tough lightweight nylon case, and a molded clip that allows the tool to be hung from a belt or pants pocket.

Drill Bits

Twist bits can be used to bore in both metal and wood. They come in many sizes, ranging from wire gauge to more than ½ inch wide. Some self-piloting bits have a special point for accurate drilling. Most twist bits are made from high-speed or carbon steel. For drilling stainless steel and other hard metals, choose a titanium or cobalt bit.

Spade bits have a long point and flat-edged cutters and are used to cut holes in wood quickly and accurately. Other types of drill bits are available for special applications, like drilling extra-large holes for a lockset, or boring into concrete. Store drill bits so they do not bump against each other, and clean them with linseed oil to prevent rust.

Twist bit can be used in wood or metal. Drill wood at high speeds, metal at low drill speeds.

Self-piloting bit requires no center punch. Special tip reduces splintering in wood, and prevents bit from binding when drilling metal.

Carbide-tipped masonry bit can drill in concrete, cinder block or brickwork. Use low drill speed, and lubricate drill hole with water to prevent overheating.

Glass & tile bit drills smooth holes in smooth, brittle surfaces. Use low drill speed, and wear gloves and eye protection.

Drill saw has twist tip to cut entry hole, and side-cutting rasp teeth for reaming cuts in wood, plastic or light-gauge metals.

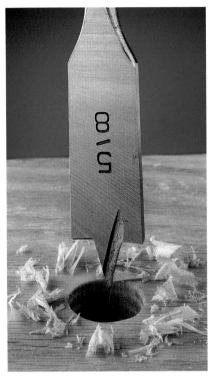

Spade bit is used to drill wood. Long tip anchors bit before the cutting edges enter the wood. Begin at low speed, gradually increasing as bit enters wood.

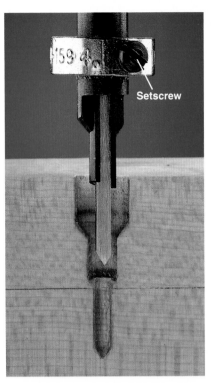

Adjustable counterbore bit drills screw pilot, countersink and counterbore holes with one action. Loosen setscrew to adjust bit to match length and shape of screw.

Plug cutter cuts circular wood plugs used to fill screw counterbore holes.

Hole saw with mandrel pilot bit cuts smooth holes in wood, like those used to mount door locksets.

Screwdriver bits, available in many styles, convert a variable-speed drill into a screwgun.

Extractor bit removes screws with worn or broken heads. Drill a pilot hole into top of screw with twist bit, then use extractor and reverse drill setting to remove screw.

Drilling Tips

Tap an indentation in wood or metal with a center punch. Starting point keeps drill bit from wandering.

Cover drilling area on glass or ceramic with masking tape. Tape keeps bit from wandering on smooth surface.

Use a backer board underneath workpiece to prevent splintering when drill bit breaks through.

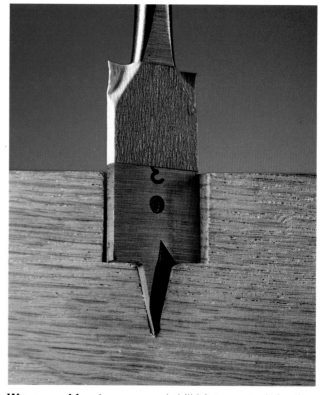

Wrap masking tape around drill bit to control depth of hole. Drill until bottom of tape is even with top of workpiece surface.

Lubricate metal with cutting oil while drilling. Oil prevents bit from overheating. Use low speed when drilling metal.

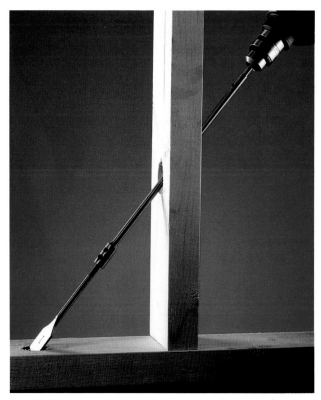

Use bit extension to drill deep or inaccessible holes. Drill at low speed until bit is fully engaged.

Prebore holes in hardwood and metal with a small bit. Preboring prevents bit from binding and wood from splintering.

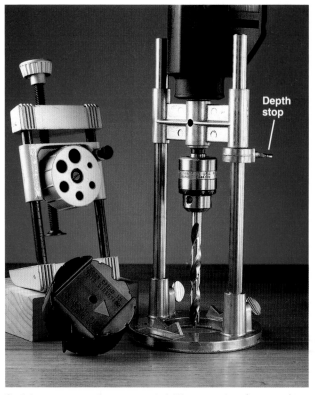

Depth stop

Guide accessories control drilling angles for precise perpendicular holes. Drill guide (right) has adjustable depth stop that controls drilling depth.

Screwdrivers & Screws

Make sure you have several hand screwdrivers, both phillips and slot types. Quality screwdrivers have hardened-steel blades and wide handles that are easy to grip.

For general use, a cordless power screwdriver saves time and effort. For frequent use, or for large jobs like installing wallboard panels, choose a power screwgun with an adjustable clutch to set screws at different depths.

Screws are categorized according to length, slot style, head shape and gauge. The thickness of the screw body is indicated by the gauge number, from 0 to 24. The larger the gauge number, the larger the screw. Large screws provide extra holding power, while small screws are less likely to split a workpiece. When joining two pieces of wood, choose a screw length so that the entire threaded portion will extend into base piece.

Where appearance is important, use countersink or counterbore bits to drill a recessed hole that will hide the screw head. A countersink bit lets you drive a flat-head screw flush with the wood surface, while a counterbore bit lets you recess the screw head to hide the location with a wood plug.

Common screwdrivers include (from top): stubby model for use in cramped areas, adjustable-clutch screwgun for fastening wallboard, ratchet hand screwdriver with interchangeable bits, cordless power screwdriver with locking spindle, slot screwdriver.

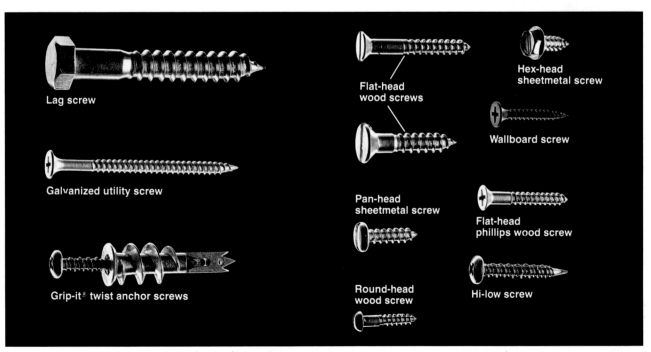

Types of screws: lag screw, galvanized utility screw, Grip-It® twist anchor screws, flat-head wood screws, pan-head sheetmetal screw, oval-head screw, hex-head sheetmetal screw, wallboard screw, flat-head phillips wood screw, hi-low screw.

Tips for Driving Screws

Lubricate screws with beeswax to make driving easier. Do not use soap, oil or grease to lubricate, because they can stain wood and corrode screws.

Pilot hole keeps wood from splitting when screw is driven. Use a twist bit with diameter that is slightly less than diameter of threaded portion of screw.

Concrete anchors

Lead anchors

Plastic concrete anchors

To install a wall anchor, drill a pilot hole in wall equal in diameter to plastic anchor. Insert anchor and drive it flush with wall. Inserted screw will expand anchor for strong, durable hold.

Use masonry & wall anchors for attaching to plaster, concrete or brick. Choose an anchor that is equal in length to the thickness of the wall surface.

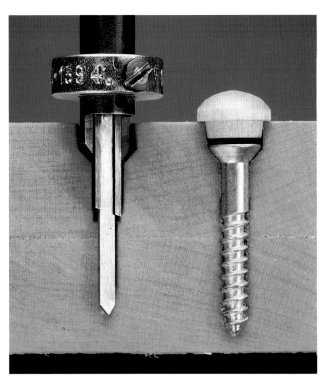

Drill counterbore pilot holes with adjustable counter-bore bit. Loosen setscrew and set bit to match length and shape of wood screw. Tighten setscrew and drill until collar reaches surface of workpiece. After driving screw, cover hole with wood plug or putty.

Utility wallboard screws have wedge-shaped heads that are self-countersinking. Wallboard screws are de-signed so they will not split wood. Use black screws for inside jobs, and galvanized screws for exterior work.

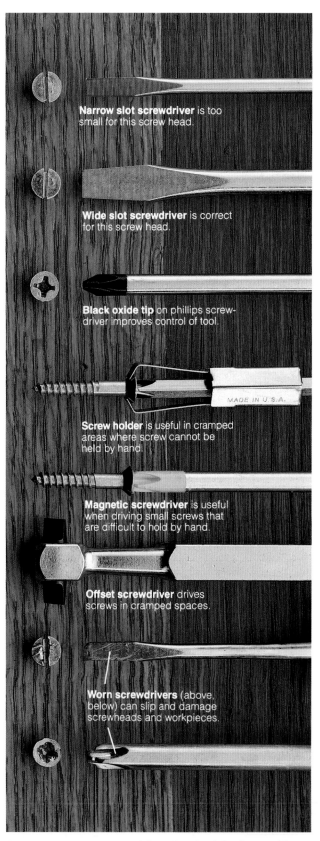

Narrow slot screwdriver is too small for this screw head.

Wide slot screwdriver is correct for this screw head.

Black oxide tip on phillips screw-driver improves control of tool.

Screw holder is useful in cramped areas where screw cannot be held by hand.

MADE IN U.S.A.

Magnetic screwdriver is useful when driving small screws that are difficult to hold by hand.

Offset screwdriver drives screws in cramped spaces.

Worn screwdrivers (above, below) can slip and damage screwheads and workpieces.

Choose proper screwdriver for the job. Screwdriver should fit slot tightly. Common types of screwdrivers include: slot, phillips, phillips with black oxide tip, screw holder, magnetic, and offset screwdrivers.

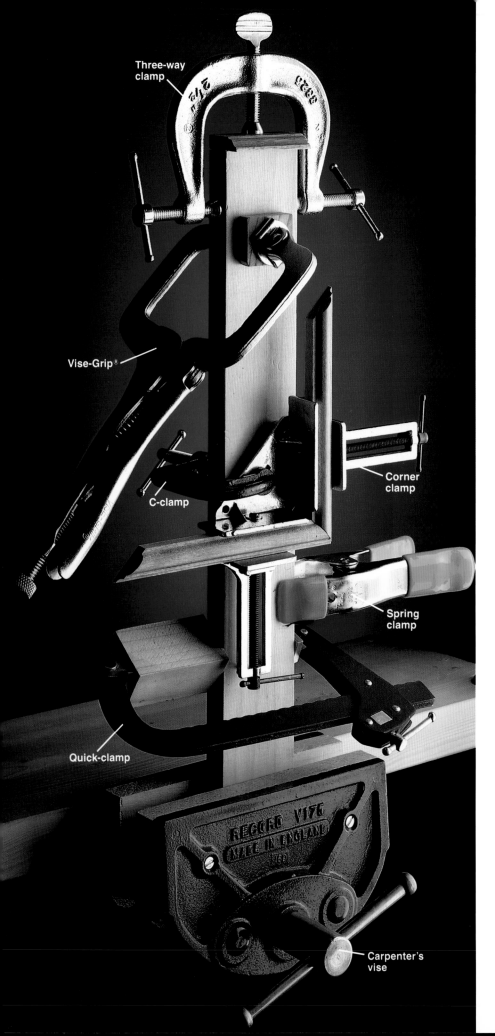

Three-way clamp

Vise-Grip®

C-clamp

Corner clamp

Spring clamp

Quick-clamp

Carpenter's vise

Clamps, Vises & Adhesives

Use vises and clamps to hold materials in place while working. Equip a workbench with a heavy-duty carpenter's vise. Clamps for small jobs include C-clamps, Vise-Grip® clamps, handscrews, and quick clamps. Clamps with metal jaws can damage a workpiece, so use scrap wood blocks between the workpiece and the clamp jaws.

For wide clamping jobs, use pipe clamps or bar clamps. The jaws of pipe clamps are connected by ordinary steel pipe. The distance between the jaws is limited only by the length of the pipe.

Adhesives bond many materials that cannot easily be nailed or screwed together, like concrete or steel. They also can reduce the number of fasteners needed to install wallboard or paneling. Many new adhesives are resistant to moisture and temperature changes, making them suitable for exterior use.

Common adhesives include (clockwise from top right): clear adhesive caulk for sealing cracks in damp areas, waterproof construction adhesive, multi-purpose adhesive, electric hot glue gun with glue sticks, yellow wood glue, white wood glue, and white all-purpose glue.

Joist & deck adhesive makes for a stronger, squeak-free floor or deck. Make sure that adhesive is waterproof for outdoor applications.

Carpenter's vise attaches to workbench to hold materials for cutting, shaping or sanding. Cover the broad jaws with hardwood to protect workpieces.

Electric hot glue gun melts glue sticks for both temporary and permanent bonding of wood and a variety of other materials.

Handscrews are wooden clamps with two adjusting screws. Handscrews are used to hold materials together while gluing. The wide wooden jaws will not damage workpiece surfaces. Handscrews adjust to fit angled workpieces.

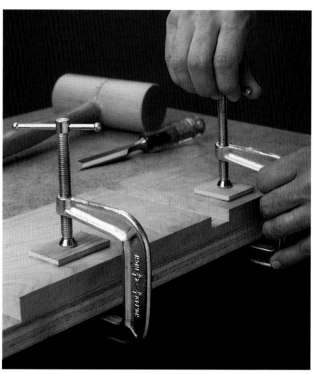

C-clamps range in clamping capacity from 1 to 6". To protect the workpiece, place scrap wood blocks between the jaws and the workpiece surface.

Corner clamp holds mitered corners when gluing picture frame moldings. Glue and clamp opposite corners, and let them dry before gluing the remaining corners.

Three-way clamp has three thumbscrews, and is used to hold edge moldings to the side of a shelf, tabletop or other flat surface. Use scraps of wood to protect workpiece surfaces.

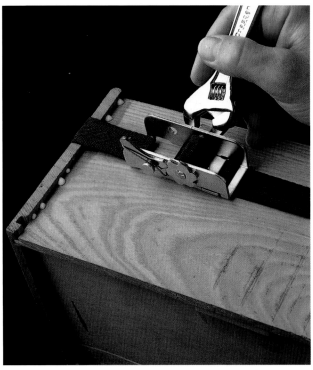

Strap clamp and white carpenter's glue are used for gluing furniture and other wood projects. Use yellow glue for exterior projects. Clamp the pieces together until the glue dries.

Pipe clamps or bar clamps hold large workpieces. Buy pipe clamp jaws in pairs to fit either ½-inch or ¾-inch diameter pipe. Clamping irregular shapes may require clamping jigs made from scrap lumber.

Workmate® portable gripping bench has a jointed, adjustable table that tightens to clamp a workpiece. Accessories, like bench stops, increase the gripping bench's versatility.

Vise-Grip® clamps provide good holding power and are easily adjusted. The hand-grip closing action makes these clamps quicker to use than traditional C-clamps.

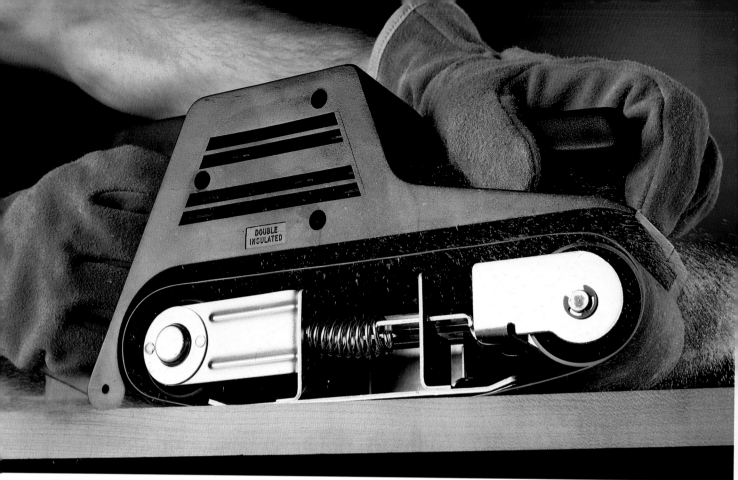

Sand large areas quickly with a belt sander. Disposable belts are available in grits ranging from 36 (extra-coarse) to 100 (fine).

Sanding

Power sanding tools and sandpaper shape and smooth wood and other building materials. For very large areas, like hardwood floors, use a high-speed floor belt sander. Portable belt sanders are suitable for most work involving rough, fast removal of material. Finishing sanders, sometimes called orbital sanders, are best for light to medium removal of material. For very small, intricate, or contoured areas, sand by hand with folded sandpaper or a sanding block.

Sanders come in several sizes and speed ranges. Small "quarter-sheet" sanders are compact and easy to handle. Larger "half-sheet" sanders are better for sanding large areas. High-speed sanders are best for removing large amounts of material, while lower-speed tools create a fine, smooth finish. Variable-speed sanders offer the greatest flexibility for different applications.

Sandpaper is available in a wide range of grits. The lower the grit number, the coarser the grit. Sanding is usually done in steps, proceeding from coarse-grit sandpaper to finer grits.

Hand sanding block is helpful for small surfaces. For curved areas, wrap sandpaper around a folded piece of scrap carpeting. Sandpaper conforms to shape of workpiece.

60-grit coarse sandpaper is used on hardwood flooring and to grind down badly scratched surfaces. Move sander across the grain for quickest removal.

100-grit medium sandpaper is best used for initial smoothing of wood. Move sander in direction of wood grain for smoothest surface.

150-grit fine sandpaper puts finish smoothness on wood surfaces. Use fine sandpaper to prepare wood surfaces for staining, or to smooth wallboard joints.

220-grit extra-fine sandpaper is used to smooth stained wood before varnishing, or between coats of varnish.

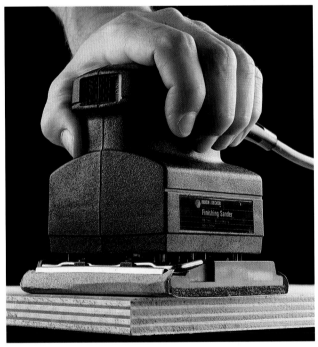

Quality finishing sanders have high-speed motors and orbital action, and can flush-sand in tight work areas. For rough-sanding, move tool across the wood grain. For smooth-finishing, move sander in same direction as wood grain.

Sanding accessories for power drills include (clockwise from top right): disc sander for fast sanding, sanding drums and flap sander to smooth contoured surfaces, and sanding drum on drill attachment.

Planes & Chisels

Shave and smooth wood with a hand plane. A hand plane has a flat cutting blade set in a steel base and is used to smooth rough surfaces or reduce the width of a piece of wood.

A wood chisel has a flat steel blade set in a handle. It cuts with light hand pressure, or by tapping the end of its handle with a mallet. A wood chisel is often used to cut hinge and lock mortises.

For best results with any shaping tool, make several shallow cuts instead of one deep cut. Forcing a tool to make deep cuts may ruin both the tool and the workpiece.

Before You Start:
Tip: For safety and ease of use, keep shaping tools sharp by honing them on an oilstone or waterstone. Choose a combination stone that has both a coarse and fine face. The stone must be soaked in water or light oil to prevent damage to the tempered metal.

How to Plane a Rough Edge

Clamp workpiece into vise. Operate plane so wood grain runs "uphill" ahead of plane. Grip toe knob and handle firmly, and plane with long, smooth strokes. To prevent dipping (overplaning at beginning and end of board), press down on toe of plane at beginning of stroke, and bear down on heel at end of stroke.

How to Chisel a Mortise

1 Mark outline of mortise with pencil. For strike-plate mortises on door frames, or for hinge mortises, use hardware as marking template when drawing outline.

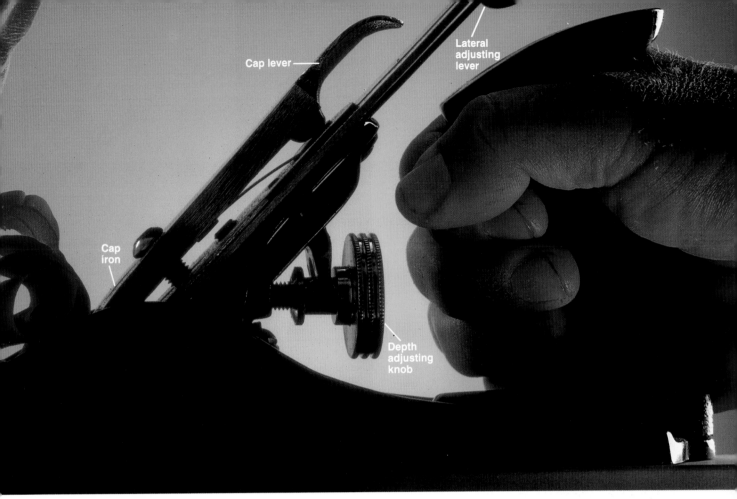

Cap lever

Lateral adjusting lever

Cap iron

Depth adjusting knob

Set plane blade depth with adjusting knob. Properly set cutter will remove wood shavings that are paper-thin. Plane may jam or gouge wood if cutter is set too deep. Use lateral adjusting lever to align cutter for an even cut. If edge of cutter leaves a score mark on wood, check lateral adjustment. Loosen the cap lever to set the cap iron 1/16" back from tip of blade.

2 Cut outline of mortise. Hold chisel with bevel-side in, and tap butt end lightly with mallet until cut is at proper depth.

3 Make a series of parallel depth cuts 1/4" apart across mortise, with chisel held at 45° angle. Drive chisel with light mallet blows to butt end of chisel.

4 Lever out waste chips by holding chisel at a low angle with bevel-side toward work surface. Drive chisel by light hand pressure.

Router

Cut decorative shapes, make grooves, and trim laminates with a router. A router is a high-speed power tool that uses changeable bits to perform a variety of cutting and shaping tasks. Because a router runs at speeds up to 25,000 revolutions per minute, it can make very smooth cuts in even the hardest woods.

For best results, make a series of routing passes, gradually extending the bit until cut reaches the correct depth. Experiment to find the proper speed for moving the router. Pushing the tool too fast slows the motor, causing the wood to chip and splinter. Moving it too slowly can scorch the wood.

Choose a router with a motor rated at 1 horsepower or more. Safety features may include a conveniently placed ON/OFF trigger switch, clear plastic chip guard, and a built-in work light.

Tip: Router bits spin in a clockwise direction, so the tool has a tendency to drift to the left. For best control, feed the router from left to right so that the cutting edge of the bit feeds into the wood.

Decorative edging is usually made with a bit that has a pilot at the tip. The round pilot rides against the edge of the workpiece to control the cut.

Common Router Bits

Corner rounding bit makes simple finish edges on furniture and wood moldings.

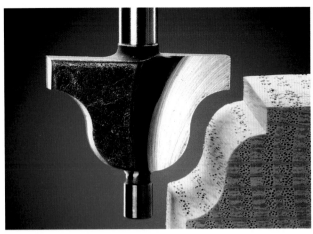

Ogee bit cuts a traditional, decorative shape in wood. Ogee bits are often used to create wood moldings and to shape the edges of furniture components.

Rabbet bit makes step-cut edges. Rabbeted edges are often used for woodworking joints and for picture frame moldings.

Ball-bearing pilot

Laminate trimmer bit cuts a finished edge on plastic laminate installations. Ball-bearing pilot prevents bit from scorching face of laminate.

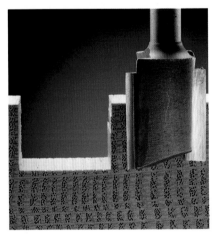

Straight bit cuts a square, flat-bottomed groove. Use it to make woodworking joints, or for free-hand routing.

Dovetail bit cuts wedge-shaped grooves used to make interlocking joints for furniture construction and cabinetwork.

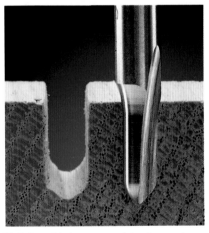

Veining bit is a round-bottomed cutter used for free-hand decorative carving and lettering.

Accessories

A few common accessories can make your work quicker and easier. A tabletop bench grinder with abrasive wheels helps clean and sharpen tools. A tool belt with pockets keeps tools and materials handy. An extension cord with multiple receptacles extends the mobility of your power tools.

A small portable tool table can make a jig saw or router more convenient to use. The tool table lets you securely mount a router or jig saw upside down, and has an adjustable edge fence and a miter guide to improve the accuracy of the tools.

Bench grinder accepts different abrasive wheels for grinding, polishing, or sharpening tools. Keep eye shields in place and wear additional eye protection when using bench grinder.

Electronic stud finder detects studs inside wall, and pinpoints both edges of the framing member. Red light comes on when the tool senses changes in wall density caused by underlying stud.

Multi-receptacle extension cord lets you plug in several power tools at the same location. To prevent electrical shock, use an extension cord that has a ground-fault circuit interrupter (GFCI).

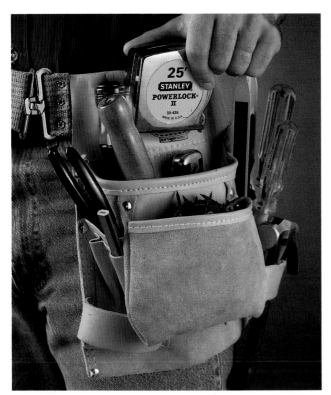

Tool belt with pockets and hammer hook keeps nails, screws and small tools handy. Wide, web belt is most comfortable for extended wear.

Portable tool table makes a jig saw or router more stable. The adjustable edge fence improves control of shaping cuts. Make sure tool table is held firmly to tabletop or workbench.

Hammer drill combines impact action with rotary motion for quick boring in concrete and masonry. To minimize dust and to keep bits from overheating, lubricate the drill site with water. A hammer drill can also be used for conventional drilling when the motor is set for rotary action only.

Tools for Special Jobs

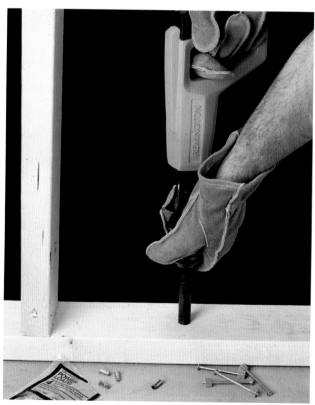

For one-time jobs or large projects, you may be able to rent or borrow special tools to make the work easier. For example, to frame a room addition or storage shed, rent an air-powered nailer that sinks framing nails with a squeeze of the trigger. Tool rental costs only a few dollars an hour, and can save hours of effort.

If you regularly work on a variety of home carpentry projects, consider buying additional power tools. For the home remodeler, a reciprocating saw is often useful. For fine woodworking and finish carpentry, a power miter box cuts angles quickly and accurately. For all-around carpentry and frequent use, invest in a table saw.

Stud driver fires a small gunpowder charge that propels masonry nails into concrete or brick. Use a stud driver to anchor a sole plate to a concrete floor.

Table saw and other stationary power tools provide greater capacity and accuracy for frequent carpentry and woodworking projects.

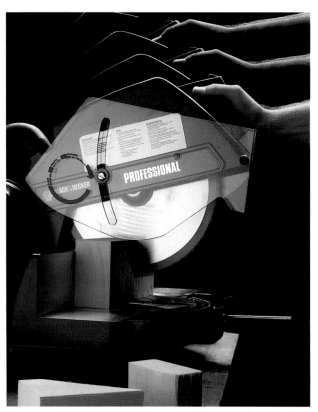

Power miter box cuts trim molding quickly and accurately. Locking motor assembly rotates up to 47° in both directions.

Air-powered nailer or stapler is attached to an air compressor. Tool trigger releases a burst of air to drive nails or staples into wood.

Reciprocating saw can be used for making cutouts in walls or floors, where a circular saw will not work, or for cutting metals like cast-iron plumbing pipes.

Check lumber visually before using it. Stored lumber can warp from temperature and humidity changes.

Lumber

Lumber for construction is usually milled from strong softwoods and is categorized by grade, moisture content, and dimension.

Grade: Characteristics such as knots, splits, and slope of the grain affect the strength of the lumber and determine the grade.

Lumber Grading Chart

Grade	Description, uses
SEL STR or select structural 1,2,3	Good appearance, strength and stiffness. 1,2,3 grades indicate knot size
CONST or Construction STAND or Standard	Both grades used for general framing, good strength and serviceability
STUD or Stud	Special designation used in any stud application, including load-bearing walls
UTIL or Utility	Used for economy in blocking and bracing

Moisture content: Lumber is also categorized by moisture content. S-DRY (surfaced dry) is the designation for lumber with a moisture content of 19% or less. S-DRY lumber is the least likely to warp or shrink and is a good choice for framing walls. S-GRN (surfaced green) means the lumber contains a moisture content of 19% or more.

Exterior lumber: Lumber milled from redwood or cedar is naturally resistant to decay and insect attack, and makes a good choice for exterior applications. The most durable part of a tree is the heartwood, so specify heartwood for wood that will be in contact with the ground.

Lumber injected with chemicals under pressure is resistant to decay. Pressure-treated lumber is generally less expensive than redwood or cedar. For outdoor structures like decks, use pressure-treated

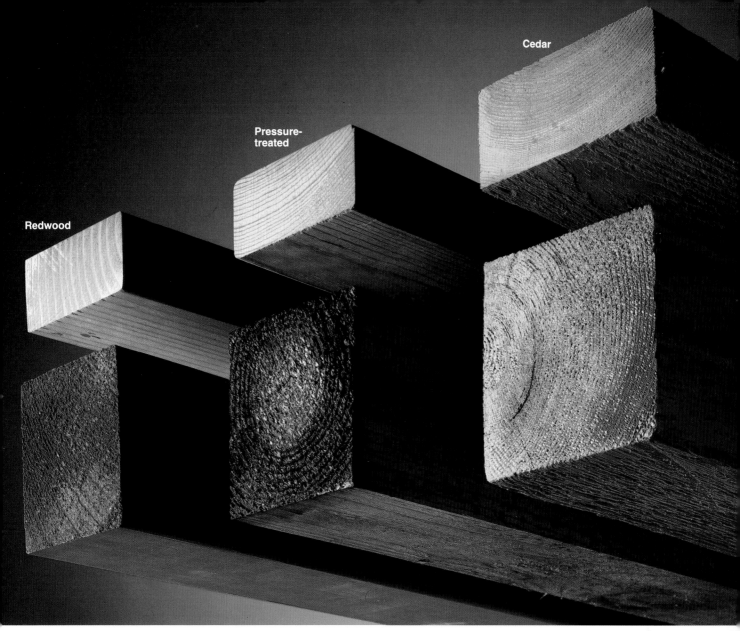

Redwood

Pressure-treated

Cedar

Build longer-lasting outdoor structures by using redwood, pressure-treated lumber or cedar. Redwood and cedar are more attractive, but pressure-treated lumber is less expensive. All are available in common lumber dimensions. Pressure-treated lumber contains toxic chemicals, so wear gloves and a protective particle mask when working with these products.

lumber for posts and joists, and more attractive redwood or cedar for decks and railings.

Dimension: Lumber is sold according to nominal sizes common throughout the industry, such as 2 × 4 and 2 × 6. The actual size of the lumber is smaller than the nominal size.

Nominal vs. Actual Lumber Dimensions

Nominal	Actual
1 × 4	¾" × 3½"
1 × 6	¾" × 5½"
1 × 8	¾" × 7½"
2 × 4	1½" × 3½"
2 × 6	1½" × 5½"
2 × 8	1½" × 7¼"

How to Read Lumber Markings

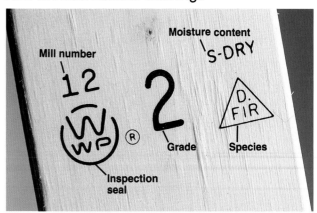

Mill number · Moisture content · S-DRY · 12 · WWP ® · 2 · Grade · Species · D. FIR · Inspection seal

Check grade stamp on lumber for grade, moisture content and species.

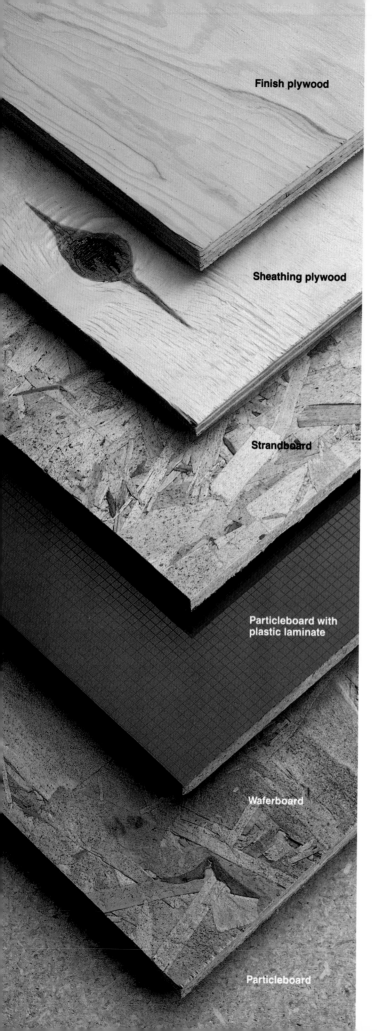

Finish plywood

Sheathing plywood

Strandboard

Particleboard with plastic laminate

Waferboard

Particleboard

Plywood & Sheet Goods

Plywood is a versatile building material made by laminating thin layers or "plies" of wood together and forming them into panels. Plywood is available in thicknesses ranging from ³⁄₁₆ to ¾ inch.

Plywood is graded A through D, according to the quality of the wood used on its outer plies. It is also graded for interior or exterior usage. Plywood is classified by group numbers, based on the wood species used for the face and back veneers. Group 1 species are the strongest and stiffest, Group 2 the next strongest.

Finish plywood may have a quality wood veneer on one side and a utility-grade ply on the other side. This will be graded A-C. If it has a quality veneer on *both* sides, the grade will be A-A.

Sheathing plywood is for structural use. It may have large knotholes that make it unsuitable for finish purposes. Sheathing plywood is rated for thickness, and is graded C-D with two rough sides. Sheathing plywood has a waterproof bond. Plywood rated EXPOSURE 1 is for use where some moisture is present. Plywood rated EXTERIOR is used in applications that are permanently exposed to weather. Sheathing plywood also carries a thickness rating and a roof and floor span index, which

How to Read Finish Plywood Markings

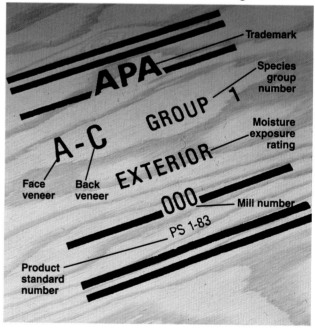

Trademark

Species group number

Moisture exposure rating

Mill number

Face veneer

Back veneer

Product standard number

Finish plywood grading stamp shows the grade of face and back veneers, species group number, and a moisture exposure rating. Mill numbers and product numbers are for manufacturer's use.

appear as two numbers separated by a diagonal slash. The first number, for roofing applications, indicates the widest allowable spacing for rafters. The second number indicates the widest spacing for joists when plywood is used for subflooring.

Strand-, particle-, and waferboards are made from waste chips or inexpensive wood species.

Plastic laminates, like Formica®, are durable, attractive surfaces for countertops and furniture. Particleboard is strong and dimensionally stable, making it an ideal base for plastic laminates.

Plastic foam insulating board is light in weight and provides good insulation for basement walls.

Water-resistant wallboard is made for use in high-moisture areas, like behind ceramic wall tiles.

Wallboard, also known as drywall, Sheetrock®, and plasterboard, comes in panels 4 feet wide by 8, 10, or 12 feet long, and in ⅜-, ½-, and ⅝-inch thicknesses.

Pegboards and hardboards like Masonite® are made from wood fibers and resins bonded together under high pressure.

How to Read Sheathing Plywood Markings

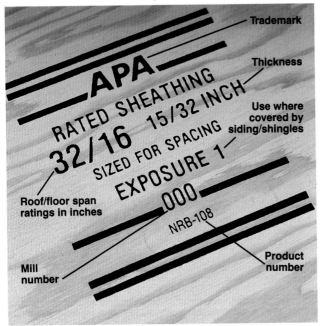

Sheathing plywood grading stamp shows thickness, roof or floor span index and exposure rating, in addition to manufacturer's information.

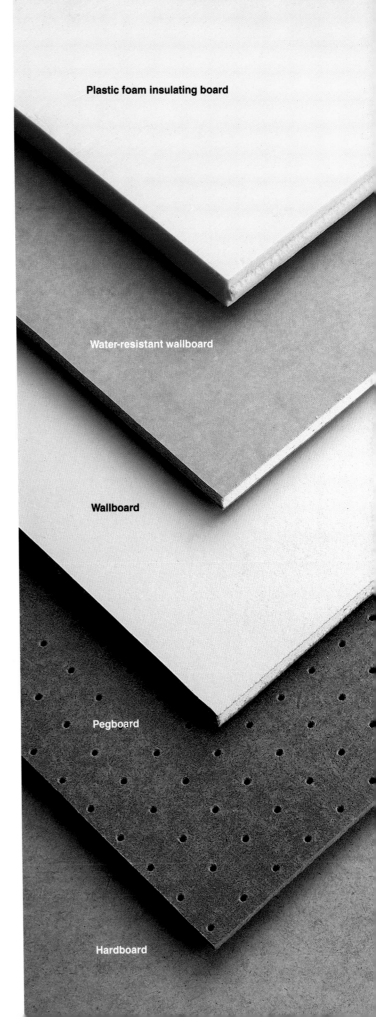

After

Header made
from two
pieces of
MicroLam®

Post

Post

Spacing
blocks

Spacing
blocks

Nailing strip

Before

Load-bearing wall

When removing a wall, first tear off the wall surface, exposing the framing members. Do not cut
wall studs until you know if you are working with a
load-bearing wall, or a non-load-bearing (partition)
wall. If the wall is load-bearing, you will need to
install temporary supports (pages 56 to 59) while
cutting out the studs. When removing a load-bearing
wall, you must replace it with a permanent header
and posts strong enough to carry the structural
weight once borne by the wall. The posts will be hid-
den inside the adjacent walls after the wallboard is
patched. The header will be visible, but covering it
with wallboard will help it blend in with the ceiling.
NOTE: Load-bearing walls more than 12 ft. long
should be removed only by a professional.

Removing & Building Walls

Removing an existing wall or building a new wall are easy ways to create more usable space without the expense of building an addition. By removing a wall, you can turn two small rooms into a large space perfect for family living. By adding new walls in a larger area, you can create a private space to use as a quiet study or as a new bedroom for a growing family.

The techniques for removing a wall vary greatly, depending on the location and the structural function of the wall. Partition walls are relatively easy to work with, while load-bearing walls require special planning.

In addition to defining living areas and supporting the house structure, walls also hold the essential mechanical systems that run through your home. You will need to consider how your project affects electrical wiring, plumbing pipes, gas pipes, and heating and air-conditioning ductwork. Unless you are confident of your own skills, it is a good idea to have a professional make changes to these systems.

Included in this section:

- Removing a wall (pages 60 to 61)
- Installing a permanent header (pages 62 to 63)
- Building a partition wall (pages 64 to 67)

Materials for Building a Header

Beam made from 2 × 12s and plywood: 8-ft. maximum recommended span

Double 9 1/2" MicroLam® beam: 10-ft. maximum recommended span. MicroLam framing members are made from thin layers of wood laminate glued together.

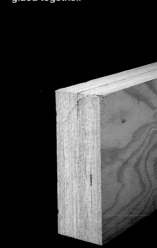

Double 11 3/8" MicroLam® beam: 11-ft maximum recommended span

12" GlueLam® beam: 12-ft. maximum recommended span. GlueLam beams are made from layers of dimension lumber laminated together. GlueLam beans can be stained and left exposed for an attractive appearance.

Manufactured support members are stronger and more durable than 2" dimension lumber, so they work well for building a header to replace a load-bearing wall. *Always consult your building inspector or a professional builder* when choosing materials and sizes for a support header.

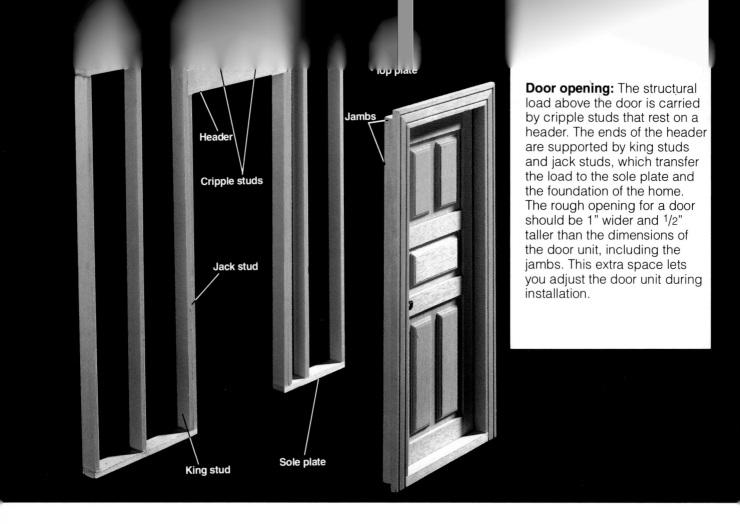

Header

Cripple studs

Top plate

Jambs

Jack stud

King stud

Sole plate

Door opening: The structural load above the door is carried by cripple studs that rest on a header. The ends of the header are supported by king studs and jack studs, which transfer the load to the sole plate and the foundation of the home. The rough opening for a door should be 1" wider and $1/2$" taller than the dimensions of the door unit, including the jambs. This extra space lets you adjust the door unit during installation.

Anatomy of Window & Door Openings

Many remodeling projects, like installing new doors or windows, require that you cut one or more studs in a load-bearing wall to create an opening. When planning your project, remember that the wall openings will require a permanent support beam, called a header, to carry the structural load directly above the removed studs.

The required size for the header is set by the Building Code, and varies according to the width of the rough opening. For a window or door opening, a header can be built from two pieces of 2" dimension lumber sandwiched around $3/8$" plywood (chart, right). When a large portion of a load-bearing wall (or the entire wall) is removed, a laminated beam product can be used to make the new header (page 53).

If you will be cutting more than one stud, make temporary supports to carry the structural load until the header is installed (pages 56 to 59).

Recommended Header Sizes

Rough Opening Width	Recommended Header Construction
Up to 3 ft.	$3/8$" plywood between two 2 x 4s
3 ft. to 5 ft.	$3/8$" plywood between two 2 x 6s
5 ft. to 7 ft.	$3/8$" plywood between two 2 x 8s
7 ft. to 8 ft.	$3/8$" plywood between two 2 x 10s

Recommended header sizes shown above are suitable for projects where a full story and roof are located above the rough opening. This chart is intended for rough estimating purposes only. For actual requirements, contact an architect or your local building inspector. For spans greater than 8 ft., see page 53.

Window opening: The structural load above the window is carried by cripple studs resting on a header. The ends of the header are supported by king studs and jack studs, which transfer the load to the sole plate and the foundation of the home. The rough sill, which helps anchor the window unit but carries no structural weight, is supported by cripple studs. To provide room for adjustments during installation, the rough opening for a window should be 1" wider and 1/2" taller than the window unit, including the jambs.

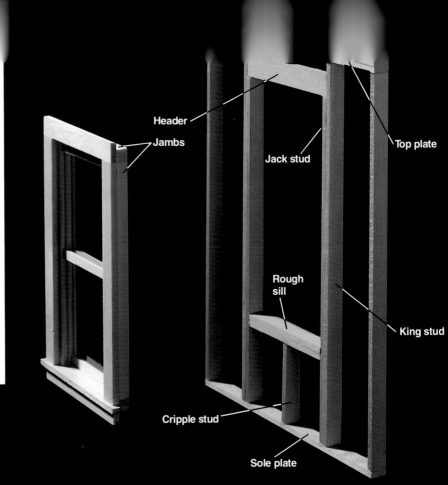

Header

Jambs

Jack stud

Top plate

Rough sill

King stud

Cripple stud

Sole plate

Framing Options for Window & Door Openings (new lumber shown in yellow)

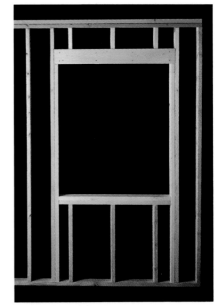

Use an existing opening to avoid new framing work. This is a good option in homes with masonry exteriors, which are difficult to alter. Order a replacement unit that is 1" narrower and 1/2" shorter than the rough opening.

Enlarge an existing opening to simplify the framing work. In many cases you can use an existing king stud and jack stud to form one side of the enlarged opening.

Frame a new opening when installing a window or door where none existed, or when replacing a smaller unit with one that is much larger.

Temporary top plate

Sole plate: found only in platform framing

Temporary sole plate

Hydraulic jacks

Temporary supports for a platform-framed house must support the ceiling joists, since the ceiling platform carries the load of the upstairs structure. Platform framing can be identified by the sole plate to which the wall studs are nailed.

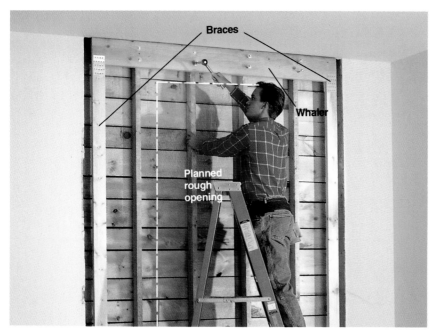

Braces

Whaler

Planned rough opening

Temporary supports for a balloon-framed house support the wall studs, which carry the upstairs load. The temporary support header, called a whaler, is anchored to the wall studs above the planned rough opening, and is supported by wall studs and bracing adjacent to the rough opening. Balloon framing can be identified by long wall studs that pass uncut through the floor to a sill plate resting on the foundation.

Remodeling Basics
Making Temporary Supports

If your project requires you to remove more than one stud in a load-bearing wall, temporary supports will be needed while you do the framing. The techniques for making temporary supports vary, depending on whether your house uses platform framing or balloon framing (see photos, left, and page 69).

Platform framing is found in most homes built after 1930. To make temporary supports, use hydraulic jacks (page opposite) or a temporary stud wall (page 58). The stud wall method is the better choice if the supports must remain in place for more than one day.

If the ceiling and floor joists run parallel to the wall you are working on, use the method shown at the bottom of page 58.

Balloon framing is found in many homes built before 1930. To make temporary supports for balloon framing, use the method shown on page 59.

Some remodeling jobs require two temporary supports. For example, when making a large opening in an interior load-bearing wall, you must install supports on both sides of the wall (page 60).

Everything You Need:

Tools: tape measure, circular saw, hammer, ratchet, drill and spade bit, hydraulic jacks.

Materials: 2 x 4 lumber, 3" lag screws, 2" utility screws, 10d nails, cloths.

How to Support Platform Framing with Hydraulic Jacks when Joists Are Perpendicular to Wall

1 Measure width of planned rough opening, and add 4 ft. so temporary support will reach well past rough opening. Cut three 2 × 4s to that length. Nail two of the 2 × 4s together with 10d nails to make a top plate for temporary support. The remaining 2 × 4 will be the sole plate for the temporary support. Place the temporary sole plate on the floor 3 ft. from the wall, centering it on the planned rough opening.

2 Set hydraulic jacks on the temporary sole plate, 2 ft. in from the ends. (Use three jacks if opening will be more than 8 ft. wide.) For each jack, build a post by nailing together a pair of 2 × 4s. Posts should be about 4" shorter than the distance between the ceiling and the top of the jacks. Attach the posts to the top plate, 2 ft. from the ends, using countersunk lag screws.

Direction of joists

3 Cover the top of the plate with a thick layer of cloth to protect the ceiling from cracking, then lift the support structure onto the hydraulic jacks.

4 Adjust the support structure so the posts are exactly plumb, then raise the hydraulic jacks until the top plate just begins to lift the ceiling. Do not lift too far, or you may damage the floor and ceiling.

Alternate: How to Support Platform Framing with a Temporary Stud Wall (Joists Perpendicular to Wall)

Joists

1 Build a 2 × 4 stud wall that is 4 ft. wider than the planned wall opening and 1³/4" shorter than the distance from floor to ceiling.

2 Raise the stud wall up and position it 3 ft. from the wall, centered on the planned rough opening.

3 Slide a 2 × 4 top plate between temporary wall and ceiling. Check to make sure wall is plumb, then drive shims under the top plate at 12" intervals until the wall is wedged tightly in place.

How to Support Platform Framing when Joists Are Parallel to Wall

Joists

2 × 4 sole plate

1 Follow directions on page 57, except: Build two 4-ft.-long cross braces, using pairs of 2 × 4s nailed together. Attach the cross braces to the double top plate, 1ft. from the ends, using countersunk lag screws.

2 Place a 2 × 4 sole plate directly over a floor joist, then set hydraulic jacks on the sole plate. For each jack, build a post 8" shorter than the jack-to-ceiling distance. Nail posts to top plate, 2 ft. from ends. Cover braces with cloth, and set support structure on jacks.

3 Adjust the support structure so the posts are exactly plumb, then pump the hydraulic jacks until the cross braces just begin to lift the ceiling. Do not lift too far, or you may damage the floor or ceiling.

How to Support Balloon Framing

1 Remove the wall surfaces around the rough opening from the floor to ceiling. Make a temporary support header (called a whaler) by cutting a 2 × 8 long enough to extend at least 20" past each side of the planned rough opening. Center the whaler against the wall studs, flush with the ceiling. Tack the whaler in place with 2" utility screws.

2 Cut two lengths of 2 × 4 to fit snugly between the bottom of the whaler and the floor. Slide 2 × 4s into place at the ends of the whaler, then attach them with nailing plates and 10d nails.

3 Drill two 3/16" holes through the whaler and into each stud it spans. Secure the whaler with 3/8" × 4" lag screws.

4 Drive shims between the bottom of each 2 × 4 and the floor to help secure the support structure.

Removing a Wall

When removing a wall, you must determine if you are working with a load-bearing wall, or a non-load-bearing (partition) wall. When removing a load-bearing wall, you will need to make temporary supports and install a header.

To maintain some separation between joined rooms, you may choose to remove just a section of the wall.

Everything You Need:

Tools: tape measure, pencil, drill and bits, reciprocating saw, pry bar, hammer.

Materials (for installing a header): 2" dimension lumber, MicroLam® framing members, 10d nails.

How to Remove a Wall

1 Prepare the project site, remove the surfaces from the wall being removed, then remove or reroute any wiring, plumbing lines, or ductwork.

2 Remove the surface of the adjoining walls to expose the permanent studs.

3 Determine if the wall being removed is load-bearing or non-load-bearing. If the wall is load-bearing, install temporary supports on each side of the wall being removed (pages 56 to 59).

4 Remove studs by cutting them through the middle and prying them away from the sole plate and top plate.

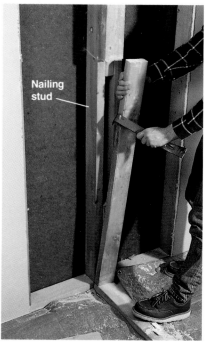

Nailing stud

5 Remove the end stud on each end of the wall. If wall being removed is load-bearing, also remove any nailing studs or blocking in the adjoining walls directly behind the removed wall.

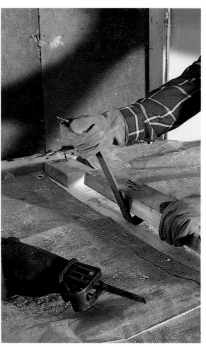

6 Make two cuts through the top plate, at least 3" apart, using a reciprocating saw or handsaw. Remove the cut section with a pry bar.

7 Remove the remaining sections of the top plate, using a pry bar.

8 Remove a 3"-wide section of sole plate, using a reciprocating saw. Pry out entire sole plate, using a pry bar. If removed wall was load-bearing, install a permanent header (page 62).

Tips for Removing a Section of Wall

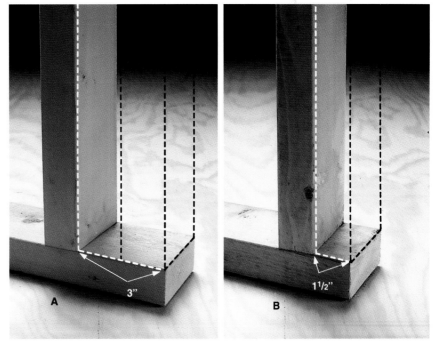

When removing wall surfaces, expose the wall back to the first permanent studs at each side of the opening.

Leave a small portion of exposed sole plate to serve as the base for posts. In a load-bearing wall (A), leave 3" of sole plate to hold the double 2 × 4 post that will support the permanent header. In a non-load-bearing wall (B), leave 1¹/₂" of exposed sole plate to hold one extra wall stud. Top plates should be removed over the entire width of the opening.

How to Install a Permanent Header when Removing a Load-bearing Wall

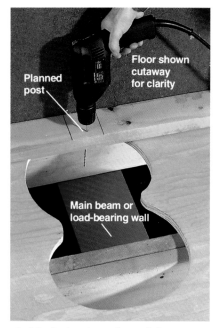

1 Mark the location of the planned support posts on the sole plate. Drill through the sole plate where support posts will rest to make sure there is a joist directly underneath. If not, install blocking under the post locations (step 2).

2 If necessary, cut and install double 2" blocking between joists. (You may need to cut into a finished ceiling to gain access to this space.) Blocking should be same size lumber as joists. Attach blocks to joists with 10d nails.

3 Build a support header to span the width of the removed wall, including the width of the support posts. See page 53 for header recommendations: in this project, the header is built with two lengths of MicroLam® joined with 10d nails.

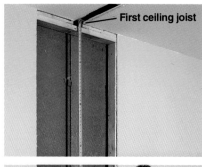

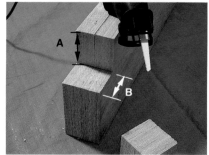

4 Lay the ends of the header on the sole plates. Find the length for each support post by measuring between the top of the header and the bottom of the first ceiling joist in from the wall.

5 Make support posts by cutting pairs of 2 × 4s to length and joining them side by side with wood glue and 10d nails.

6 Measure the thickness (A) and width (B) of the top plate at each end, then notch the top corners of the header to fit around the top plates, using a reciprocating saw.

7 Lift the header against the ceiling joists, then set the posts under the ends of the header. If the header will not fit due to sagging ceiling joists, then raise the joists by jacking up or shimming the temporary supports.

8 Toenail the posts to the header with 10d nails.

9 Check each post for plumb with a carpenter's level, and adjust it if necessary by tapping the bottom with a hammer. When post is plumb, mark a reference line on the sole plate, and toenail the bottom of each post to the sole plate.

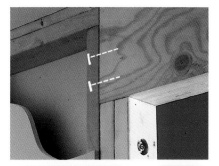

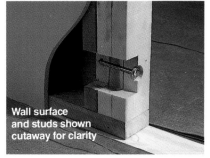

Wall surface and studs shown cutaway for clarity

10 Cut 2 × 4 nailing strips and attach them to each side of the post and header with 10d nails. Nailing strips provide a surface for attaching new wallboard.

11 Cut and toenail spacing blocks to fit into the gaps between the permanent studs and the nailing strips. Patch and finish the wall and beam.

When removing a section of a wall, attach the posts to the wall studs with countersunk lag screws (bottom). Endnail the wall studs to the header with 10d nails (top).

Building a Partition Wall

Partition walls divide spaces into rooms, but do not carry any significant structural weight. Because partition walls are not load-bearing, the framing techniques are simple. However, take care to make sure the new wall you build is plumb, straight, and perpendicular to the adjoining walls.

Interior partition walls usually are built with 2 × 4 lumber, but in some situations it is better to frame with 2 × 6 lumber (photo, left). Before finishing the walls with wallboard, have the building inspector review your work. The inspector also may check to see that any required plumbing and wiring changes are complete.

Use 2 × 6 lumber to frame a new wall that must hold large plumbing pipes. Where wall plates must be cut to fit pipes, use metal straps to join the framing members (inset). For improved soundproofing, you can also fill walls with fiberglass insulation.

Everything You Need:

Tools: drill and twist bit, chalk line, tape measure, combination square, pencil, framing square, ladder, plumb bob, hammer.

Materials: framing lumber, 10d nails.

Variations for Fastening New Walls to Joists

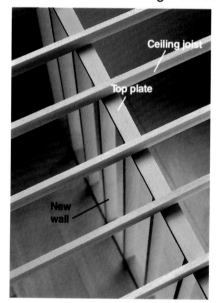

New wall perpendicular to joists: Attach the top plate and sole plate directly to the ceiling and floor joists with 10d nails.

New wall parallel to joists, but not aligned: Install 2 × 4 blocking between the joists every 2 ft., using 10d nails. Bottom of blocking should be flush with the edges of joists. Anchor plates with 10d nails driven into the blocking.

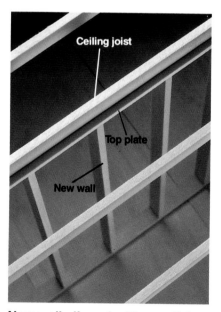

New wall aligned with parallel joists: Attach top plate to ceiling joist and sole plate to the floor, using 10d nails.

How to Build a Partition Wall

1 Mark the location of the new wall on the ceiling, then snap two chalk lines to outline the position of the new top plate. Locate the first ceiling joist or cross block by drilling into the ceiling between the lines, then measure to find the remaining joists.

2 Make the top and bottom wall plates by cutting two 2 × 4s to wall length. Lay the plates side by side, and use a combination square to outline the stud locations at 16" intervals.

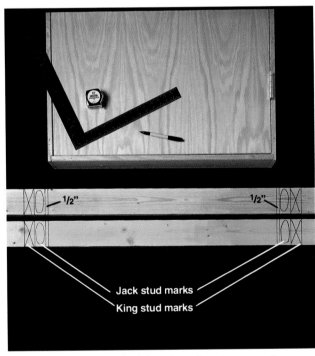

1/2"   1/2"

Jack stud marks
King stud marks

3 Mark the position of the door framing members on the top plate and sole plate, using Xs for king studs and Os for jack studs. The rough opening measured between the insides of jack studs should be about 1" wider than the actual width of the door to allow for adjustments during installation.

4 Position the top plate against the ceiling between the chalk lines, and use two 10d nails to tack it in place with the stud marks facing down. Use a framing square to make sure the plate is perpendicular to the adjoining walls, then anchor the plate to the joists with 10d nails.

(continued next page)

5 Determine position of sole plate by hanging a plumb bob from edge of the top plate near an adjoining wall so the plumb bob tip nearly touches the floor. When the plumb bob is motionless, mark its position on the floor. Repeat at the opposite end of top plate, then snap a chalk line between the marks to show the location of the sole plate edge.

6 Cut away the portion of the sole plate where the door framing will fit, then position the remaining pieces against the sole plate outline on the floor. On wood floors, anchor the sole plate pieces with 10d nails driven into the floor joists.

On concrete floors, attach the sole plate with a stud driver, available at rental centers. A stud driver fires a small gunpowder charge to drive a masonry nail through the framing member and into the concrete. Wear hearing protectors when using a stud driver.

7 Find the length of the first stud by measuring the distance between the sole plate and the top plate at the first stud mark. Add 1/8" to ensure a snug fit, and cut the stud to length.

8 Position the stud between the top plate and sole plate so the stud markings are covered.

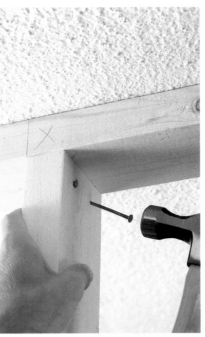

9 Attach the stud by toenailing through the sides of the studs and into the top plate and sole plate. Measure, cut, and install all remaining studs one at a time.

Option: Attach the studs to sole plate and top plate with metal connectors and 4d nails.

10 Frame the rough opening for the door (see pages 68 to 69).

11 Install 2 × 4 blocking between studs, 4 ft. from the floor. Arrange to have the wiring and any other utility work completed, then have your project inspected. Install wallboard and trim the wall.

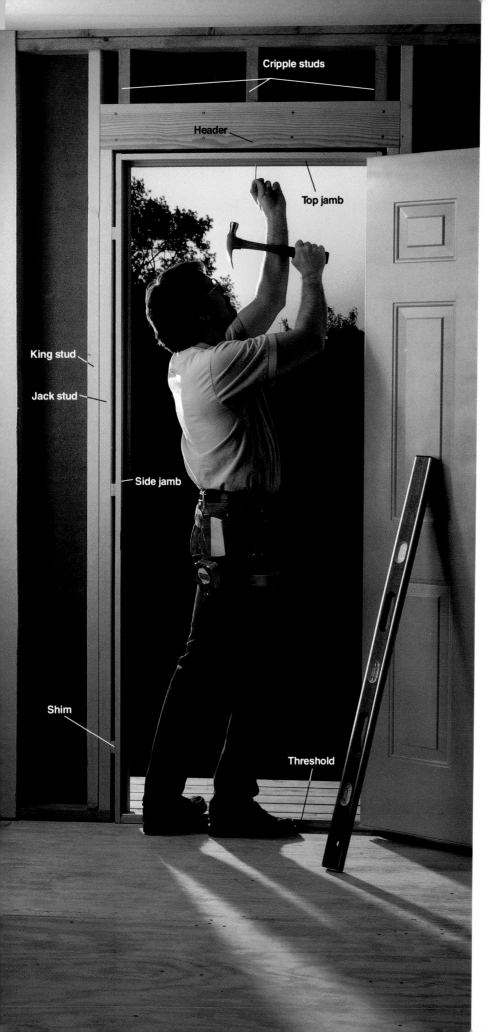

Cripple studs

Header

Top jamb

King stud

Jack stud

Side jamb

Shim

Threshold

Framing Door Openings

Your local home center carries many interior and exterior doors in stock sizes. For custom sizes, have the home center special-order the doors from the manufacturer. Special orders generally take three or four weeks for delivery.

For easy installation, buy "prehung" interior and exterior doors, which are already mounted in their jambs. Although unmounted doors are widely available, installing them is a complicated job that is best left to a professional.

When replacing an existing door, choosing a new unit the same size as the old door makes your work easier, because you can use framing members already in place.

The following pages show installation techniques for wood-frame houses with lap siding.

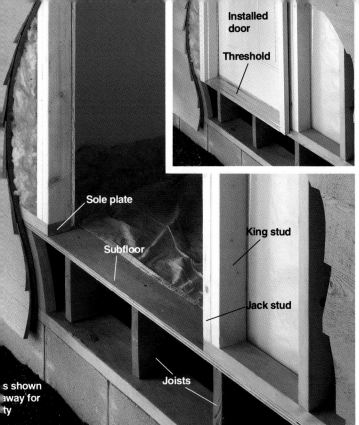

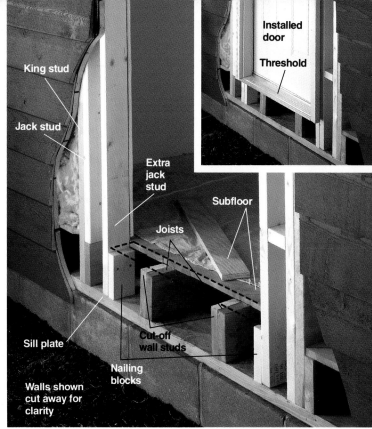

New door opening in a platform-framed house has studs that rest on a sole plate running across the top of the subfloor. The sole plate between the jack studs is cut away so the threshold for the new door can rest directly on the subfloor.

New door opening in a balloon-framed house has studs extending past the subfloor to rest on the sill plate. Jack studs rest either on the sill plate or on top of the joists. To provide a surface for the door threshold, install nailing blocks, and extend the sub-floor out to the ends of the joists, using plywood.

How to Frame a Door Opening

The rough opening for a new door should be framed after the interior preparation work is done, but before the exterior wall surfaces are removed. The methods for framing the opening will vary, depending on whether your house is built with platform framing or balloon framing (see photos, above).

Always build temporary supports to hold up the ceiling if your project requires that you cut or remove more than one stud in a load-bearing wall (pages 56 to 59).

Everything You Need:

Tools: tape measure, pencil, level, plumb bob, reciprocating saw, circular saw, hand-saw, hammer, pry bar, nippers.

Materials: 2" dimension lumber, 3/8" plywood, 10d nails.

When framing a door opening in a new wall, install the door framing members at the same time you install the wall studs (pages 64 to 67). Cut and install cripple studs to reach between the top of the header and the top plate. Cripples should be spaced at the same interval as the wall studs, and anchored with 10d nails.

How to Frame a Door Opening

1 Prepare the project site, and remove the interior wall surfaces.

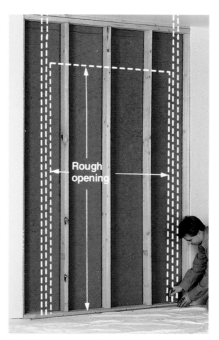

2 Measure and mark the rough opening width on the sole plate. Mark the locations of the jack studs and king studs on the sole plate. (Where practical, use existing studs as king studs.)

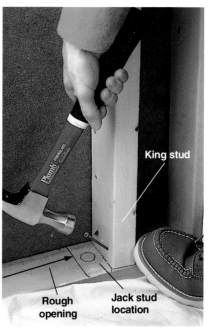

3 Measure and cut king studs to fit between the sole plate and top plate. Position the king studs and toenail them to the sole plate with 10d nails.

4 Check the king studs with a level to make sure they are plumb, then toenail them to the top plate with 10d nails.

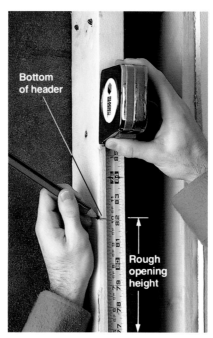

5 Measuring from the floor, mark the rough opening height on one king stud. For most doors, the recommended rough opening is 1/2" greater than the height of the door jamb. This line marks the bottom of the door header.

6 Measure and mark where the top of the header will fit against a king stud. Header size depends on the distance between the king studs (page 54). Use a level to extend the lines across the intermediate studs to the opposite king stud.

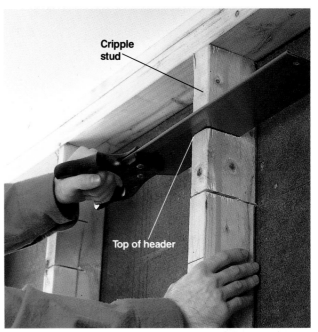

Cripple stud

Top of header

7 Cut two jack studs to reach from the top of the sole plate to the rough opening marks on the king studs. Nail the jack studs to the king studs with 10d nails driven every 12". **Make temporary supports** (pages 56 to 59) if wall is load-bearing and you are removing more than one stud.

8 Use a circular saw set to maximum blade depth to cut through the old studs that will be removed. The remaining stud sections will be used as cripple studs for the door frame. Do not cut king studs. Make additional cuts 3" below the first cuts, then finish the cuts with a handsaw.

9 Knock out the 3" stud sections, then tear out the rest of the studs with a pry bar. Clip away any exposed nails, using a nippers.

10 Build a header to fit between the king studs on top of the jack studs. Use two pieces of 2" dimension lumber sandwiched around 3/8" plywood (page 76). Attach the header to the jack studs, king studs, and cripple studs, using 10d nails.

11 Use a reciprocating saw to cut through the sole plate next to each jack stud, then remove the sole plate with a pry bar. Cut off any exposed nails or anchors, using a nippers.

How to Frame a Door Opening in a Balloon-framed House

1 Prepare the project site and remove the interior wall surfaces. Select two existing studs to use as king studs. The distance between selected studs must be at least 3" wider than the planned rough opening. Measuring from the floor, mark the rough opening height on a king stud.

2 Measure and mark where the top of the header will fit against the king stud. Header size depends on the distance between the king studs (page 54). Use a level to extend the line across the studs to the opposite king stud.

3 Use a reciprocating saw to cut open the subfloor between the studs, then remove any fire blocking in the stud cavities. This allows access to the sill plate when installing the jack studs. If you will be removing more than one wall stud, **make temporary supports** (pages 56 to 59).

4 Use a circular saw to cut studs along the lines marking the top of header. Do not cut king studs. Make two additional cuts on each cut stud, 3" below the first cut and 6" above the floor. Finish cuts with a handsaw, then knock out 3" sections with a hammer. Remove the studs with a pry bar (page 71).

5 Cut two jack studs to reach from the top of the sill plate to the rough opening mark on the king studs. Nail the jack studs to the king studs with 10d nails driven every 12".

6 Build a header to fit between the king studs on top of the jack studs, using two pieces of 2" dimension lumber sandwiched around 3/8" plywood (page 76). Attach the header to the jack studs, king studs, and cripple studs, using 10d nails.

7 Measure and mark the rough opening width on the header. Use a plumb bob to mark the rough opening on the sill plate (inset).

8 Cut and install additional jack studs, as necessary, to frame the sides of the rough opening. Toenail the jack studs to the top plate and the sill plate, using 10d nails. NOTE: You may have to go to the basement to do this.

9 Install horizontal 2 × 4 blocking, where necessary, between the studs on each side of the rough opening, using 10d nails. Blocking should be installed at the lockset location and at the hinge locations on the new door.

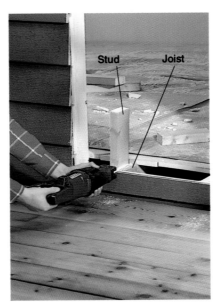

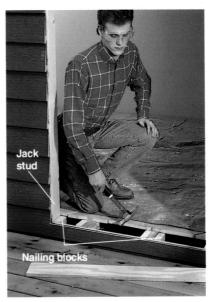

10 Remove the exterior wall surface.

11 Cut off the ends of the exposed studs flush with the tops of the floor joists, using a reciprocating saw or handsaw.

12 Install 2 × 4 nailing blocks next to the jack studs and joists, flush with the tops of the floor joists (See NOTE in Step 8). Reinstall any fire-blocking that was removed. Patch the subfloor area between the jack studs with plywood to form a flat, level surface for the door threshold.

Header

Angled stud

Jambs

Shims

Double rough sill

Insulation

Cripple studs

Jack stud

King stud

Framing Window Openings

Most good windows must be custom-ordered several weeks in advance. To save time, do the interior framing work before the window unit arrives. But never open the outside wall surface until you have the window and accessories, and are ready to install them.

Follow the manufacturer's specifications for rough opening size when framing for a window. The listed opening usually is 1" wider and 1/2" higher than the actual dimension of the window unit.

The following pages show techniques for wood-frame houses with siding. If your house has balloon framing, use the method shown on page 72 (steps 1 to 6) to install a header.

If you have masonry walls, or if you are installing polymer-coated windows, you may want to attach your windows using masonry clips instead of nails.

Everything You Need:

Tools: tape measure, pencil, combination square, hammer, level, circular saw, handsaw, pry bar, nippers, drill and bits, reciprocating saw, stapler, nail set, caulk gun.

Materials: 10d nails, 2" dimension lumber, 3/8" plywood, shims, building paper, drip edge, casing nails (16d, 8d), fiberglass insulation, silicone caulk.

How to Frame a Window Opening

1 Prepare the project site and remove the interior wall surfaces. Measure and mark rough opening width on sole plate. Mark the locations of the jack studs and king studs on sole plate. Where practical, use existing studs as king studs.

2 Measure and cut king studs, as needed, to fit between the sole plate and top plate. Position the king studs and toenail them to the sole plate with 10d nails.

3 Check the king studs with a level to make sure they are plumb, then toenail them to the top plate with 10d nails.

4 Measuring from the floor, mark the rough opening height on one of the king studs. For most windows, the recommended rough opening is 1/2" taller than the height of the window frame. This line marks the bottom of the window header.

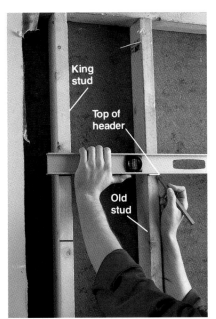

5 Measure and mark where the top of the window header will fit against the king stud. The header size depends on the distance between the king studs (page 54). Use a carpenter's level to extend the lines across the old studs to the opposite king stud.

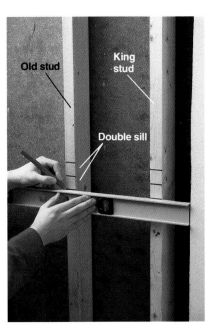

6 Measure down from header line and outline the double rough sill on the king stud. Use a carpenter's level to extend the lines across the old studs to the opposite king stud. **Make temporary supports** (pages 56 to 59) if you will be removing more than one stud.

(continued next page)

How to Frame a Window Opening (continued)

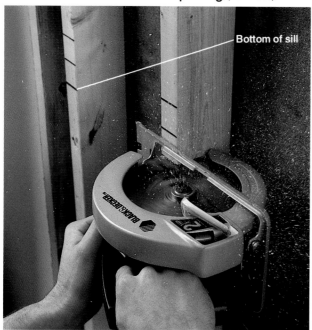

Bottom of sill

7 Use a circular saw set to maximum blade depth to cut through the old studs along the lines marking the bottom of the rough sill, and along the lines marking the top of the header. Do not cut the king studs. On each stud, make an additional cut about 3" above the first cut. Finish the cuts with a handsaw.

Top of header

Cripple studs

Bottom of sill

8 Knock out the 3" stud sections, then tear out the old studs inside the rough opening, using a pry bar. Clip away any exposed nails, using a nippers. The remaining sections of the cut studs will serve as cripple studs for the window.

Plywood

9 Build a header to fit between the king studs on top of the jack studs, using two pieces of 2" dimension lumber sandwiched around 3/8" plywood.

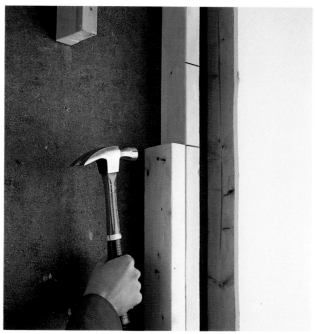

10 Cut two jack studs to reach from the top of the sole plate to the bottom header lines on the king studs. Nail the jack studs to the king studs with 10d nails driven every 12". NOTE: On a balloon-frame house the jack studs will reach to the sill plate, or only to the subfloor, if you are working on the second story (page 69).

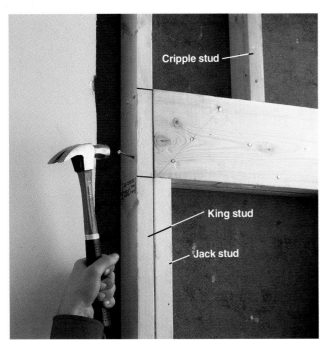

Cripple stud

King stud

Jack stud

11 Position the header on the jack studs, using a hammer if necessary. Attach the header to the king studs, jack studs, and cripple studs, using 10d nails.

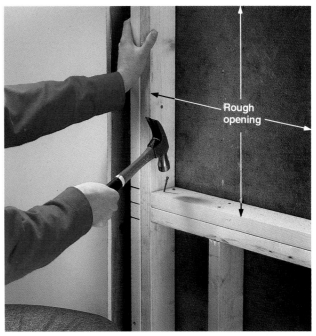

Rough opening

12 Build the rough sill to reach between the jack studs by nailing a pair of 2 × 4s together. Position the rough sill on the cripple studs, and nail it to the jack studs and cripple studs with 10d nails.

Variations for Round-top Windows

Create a template to help you mark the rough opening on the sheathing. Scribe the outline of the curved frame on cardboard, allowing an extra 1/2" for adjustments within the rough opening. A 1/4" × 1 1/4" metal washer makes a good spacer for scribing the outline. Cut out the template along the scribed line.

Marvin Windows
WARROAD, MINNESOTA
56763

Tape the template to the sheathing, with the top flush aginst the header. Use the template as a guide for attaching diagonal framing members across the top corners of the framed opening. The diagonal members should just touch the template. Outline the template on the sheathing as a guide for cutting the rough opening.

Index

Cowles Creative Publishing, Inc.
offers a variety of how-to books.
For information write:
  Cowles Creative Publishing
  Subscriber Books
  5900 Green Oak Drive
  Minnetonka, MN 55343